	Dewey	©	Price			Dewey	©	Price
Growth and Life Cycles	571	2006	$18.95		Light	535	2006	$18.95
Life Processes	612	2006	$18.95		Magnets	538	2006	$18.95
Local Wildlife	591	2006	$18.95		Rocks and Soil: Gems, Metals, and Minerals	552	2008	$18.95
Measuring: How Big Is It?	516	2008	$18.95		Space: Sun, Moon, and Stars	520	2008	$18.95
Minibeasts: Going on a Bug Hunt	590	2008	$18.95		Springs	621	2006	$18.95
Time: What Time Is It?	529	2008	$18.95					
Using Electricity	537	2006	$18.95					
Weather: Rain or Shine	551	2008	$18.95					

USA247AR2.8-3.2

USA247AR3.2-3.9

11 Vols.   **SGB1008-2**

Science Starters Level 3

Publisher **Stargazer Books**

Purchase Series & Save!
Publisher's List Price $298.10
Gumdrop Price $198.00

Library Binding
Reviews: SLJ

Title	Dewey	©	Item Price
Animal Kingdom	590	2006	$18.95
Balancing: Cranes, Scales and Seesaws	531	2008	$18.95
Conservation: Animals in Danger	333	2008	$18.95
Friction: Wheels and Brakes	531	2008	$18.95
Growing Plants: Leaves, Roots, and Shoots	630	2008	$18.95
Health and Diet	613	2006	$18.95

• prepub
Titles may be purchased individually.

Note to Parents and Teachers

The SCIENCE STARTERS series introduces key science vocabulary and concepts to young children while encouraging them to discover and understand the world around them. The series works as a set of graded readers in three levels.

LEVEL 3: READ ALONE
These books can be read alone or as part of guided or group reading. Each book has three sections:

• Information pages that introduce key concepts. Key words appear in bold for easy recognition on pages where the related science concepts are explained.
• A lively story that recalls this vocabulary and encourages children to use these words when they talk and write.
• A quiz asks children to look back and recall what they have read.

LEAVES, ROOTS, and SHOOTS looks at GROWING PLANTS. Below are some answers and activities related to the questions on the information spreads that parents, carers, and teachers can use to discuss and develop further ideas and concepts:

p. 4 *Why else do we grow plants?* As well as making our world beautiful, e.g. flowers, trees, and shrubs, plants provide us with all sorts of materials, e.g. wood, rubber, paper, corks, and charcoal come from trees; cotton comes from a bush.

p. 6 *Use pots and trays for planting seeds.* Encourage children to visit a garden to see the range of plants and to watch how tools are used by a gardener for different jobs.

p. 9 *Will the plant with the leaves picked off grow as well as the other plant?* No. You could explain that a plant is bit like a machine, e.g bicycle—all its parts need to be effective if it is going to work properly. Without its leaves, a plant cannot turn energy from the sun into the food it needs to grow healthily.

p. 14 *Too much water can kill a plant.* However, point out that some plants have adapted to living in water, e.g. rice, duckweed. Some have their roots underwater but their stems above the water, e.g. bulrush. Some have leaves floating on the surface, e.g. water lilies. Some are completely under the water—you can often see a stream of tiny bubbles coming from their leaves (e.g. some types of pondweed).

p. 19 *Why do you think a greenhouse is made of glass?* The glass roof and walls of a greenhouse keep the plants inside warm while letting light from the sun shine in.

p. 21 *Why does adding compost to soil help plants grow?* The compost adds nutrients to the soil, which helps plants grow as they absorb these nutrients through their roots.

ADVISORY TEAM

Educational Consultant
Andrea Bright—Science Coordinator, Trafalgar Junior School

Literacy Consultant
Jackie Holderness—former Senior Lecturer in Primary Education, Westminster Institute, Oxford Brookes University

Series Consultants
Anne Fussell—Early Years Teacher and University Tutor, Westminster Institute, Oxford Brookes University

David Fussell—C.Chem., FRSC

CONTENTS

© Aladdin Books Ltd 2008

Designed and produced by
Aladdin Books Ltd

First published in
the United States in 2008 by
Stargazer Books
c/o The Creative Company
123 South Broad Street
P.O. Box 227, Mankato,
Minnesota 56002

Printed in the United States
All rights reserved

Editor: Sally Hewitt
Designer: Jim Pipe
Series Design: Flick, Book
Design & Graphics

Thanks to:
The pupils of Trafalgar
Infants School for appearing as
models in this book.

**Library of Congress
Cataloging-in-Publication Data**

Pipe, Jim, 1966-
  Growing plants / by Jim Pipe.
    p. cm. -- (Science starters)
  ISBN 978-1-59604-140-0
  (alk. paper)
  1. Growth (Plants)--Juvenile
literature. 2. Gardening--
Juvenile literature. 3. Plant
propagation--Juvenile literature.
I. Title.

QK731.P584 2007
630--dc22

                2007009209

Photocredits:
*l-left, r-right, b-bottom, t-top,
c-center, m-middle*
All photos istockphoto.com
except: Cover tr, 21b—
USDA. 2tl, 9tr, 16br, 20b,
26mr—Corbis. 2bl, 4mr, 8br,
9br, 14tr, 31tr—Marc Arundale
/ Select Pictures. 4bl, 11mr,
17br, 24br, 30mr, 31br—
Ingram Publishing. 5t, 15b—
Photodisc. 12bl—Stockbyte.
22tr, 23br—Digital Vision.
24tl, 25 both, 26 both, 28 both,
29tr, 30tl, 31bcl—Jim Pipe. 27tl
—Otto Rogge Photography.

GROWING PLANTS

Leaves, Roots, and Shoots

by Jim Pipe

Stargazer Books

HEALTHY PLANTS

Flowers

Plants are living things, just like people.
They can be big trees or tiny flowers.

Some **plants** can live in cold, windy places.
Other **plants** need bright sunshine or shelter.

Like us, **plants** need lots of care.
They grow better if we look after them.

Healthy plants make healthy food for us. Visit a market to see the different vegetables, fruits, grains, and seeds we eat. Why else do we grow plants?

Though **plants** grow in many different places around the world, they all need these things to be **healthy:**

Water
Plants need water,
but not too much.

Light
Light from the sun
helps a plant make food.

Warmth
Some plants don't like
the cold. A greenhouse
keeps them warm.

Good soil
Soil gives a plant the
nutrients that help it
to grow.

IN THE GARDEN

A **garden** is a good place to grow plants. You can grow flowers or vegetables.

You can also grow plants indoors or in a windowbox.

Trowel

Fork

Tools help you to grow plants. Use a trowel for digging.

Use a fork to break the soil into crumbs. Use pots and trays for planting seeds.

An indoor garden

You can help plants grow. You have to learn how to watch and wait while they grow. It can take a long time!

Be careful in the **garden**. Always wash your hands after touching soil or plants.

Never eat anything from a **garden** without asking an adult first.

This boy is growing bean plants in his garden.

LEAVES

Here are some important parts on a plant.

Leaves

Stem

Roots

Unhealthy plant

For a plant to grow, all these parts need to be healthy.

This plant on the right is not healthy. Can you see why?

It only has a few green **leaves**. Its stem is yellow and twisted. Its roots are tangled.

8

A plant's green **leaves** make food from sunlight and water.

A **leaf's** shape helps it to catch the light. Look at the shapes of different **leaves**.

Some plants have large **leaves**. Other plants have long rows of small **leaves**.

A tree has roots and leaves like other plants. Its stem is called its trunk.

Looking at leaves

If you are doing an experiment, always use more than one plant.

You can test how leaves help a plant grow. On one plant, pick off half of the leaves. Do you think this plant will grow as well as the other one?

ROOTS

A plant takes in water through its **roots**.
Roots spread out, to get all the water they can.

Roots also grip the ground. They stop a plant
from being blown over or washed away.

Roots

Some plants don't
need deep roots.

They can grow
in bits of soil
between rocks.

A tree has lots of **roots**. Its **roots** can be four times as long as its branches!

Some **roots** can be eaten, such as carrots, parsnips, and radishes.

Radishes

Tree roots

You don't have to grow plants from seeds. Leave an old potato out in the light.

Potato

The potato will start growing roots. If you plant it in the ground it will grow a new potato plant!

STEMS AND SHOOTS

Stems carry water from the roots to the leaves. They carry food made by the leaves to other parts of the plant.

The **stems** of ivy plants cling to walls and trees. A strong **stem** helps some plants to reach up toward the sun, like these corn plants.

Ivy

Corn plants

Not all **stems** grow upward. The **stem** of a strawberry plant runs along the ground.

Strawberry plants

When a **stem** first begins to grow from the roots, it is called a **shoot**.

Shoot

The stem is the longest part of many plants. If you are growing a plant, try to measure it as it grows.

Make sure you always measure in the same way—from the soil to the very top of the plant.

Adult tulip

Tulip shoot

13

WATER

All plants need **water**. Without **water**, the leaves turn brown and a plant dies.

Check your plants twice a week to see if they need **water**.

Poke your finger into the soil. If the soil feels dry, **water** your plant. Then wash your hands.

Testing soil

Be careful! Plants also need air. Too much water stops the air reaching the roots. It can kill a plant.

Some plants like to grow in or near **water**. Beautiful flowers and reeds grow in ponds and lakes.

Other plants can grow with very little **water**. Some grasses can grow on a sandy beach. A cactus can grow in a desert.

Water lilies

Cactus

LIGHT

Plants need **light** to help them grow. If you are growing a plant indoors, put it near a window.

A plant can tell you when it isn't getting enough **light**. Its stem will be thin. It will lean toward the **light**.

Don't put indoor plants in the sun. Their leaves can get burnt.

Sunflowers turn their heads to follow the sun.

16

Campsite

When a plant does not get enough **light**, its leaves turn yellow.

Look at the grass above. There is a yellow patch where a tent has cut off the **light**.

After a few days in the **light**, the grass will turn green again. This shows it is healthy.

Put a plant in a dark closet for a few days and see what happens when it does not get enough light.

WARMTH

Like us, plants like to be not too hot, and not too cold. Find out where your plants come from so you know how to make them feel at home.

Plants from the rainforest like **warm** weather. Mountain flowers like cooler weather.

Rainforest plants

Mountain plants

Too much heat is bad
for most plants.
A hot summer turns
the grass yellow.

Very cold weather is
also bad for plants.
In spring, a bad frost
can kill young plants.

Frost on a leaf

Greenhouse

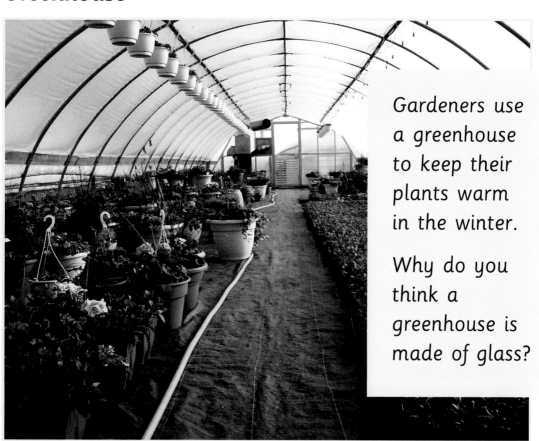

Gardeners use
a greenhouse
to keep their
plants warm
in the winter.

Why do you
think a
greenhouse is
made of glass?

SOIL

Good **soil** helps plants to grow. The **soil** contains chemicals, called nutrients. A plant soaks up the nutrients through its roots.

When you plant seeds, use a fork to break up the **soil**. Crumbly **soil** makes it easier for seeds to grow.

Some plants get nutrients from animals! A Venus flytrap has leaves that snap shut, catching minibeasts inside.

Good soil

This boy is testing which **soils** are good for plants. He puts a small plant in 3 pots.

One pot is full of crumbly **soil**. One is full of sand. One is full of stony **soil**.

He gives each plant the same amount of light and water. Which plant do you think will grow best?

Compost is made from rotting grass and dead leaves. It is full of nutrients.

Why does adding compost to soil help plants grow?

PESTS AND WEEDS

Plants are also food for other living things. Caterpillars and snails love to munch plants.

If you want to get rid of minibeast **pests**, spray your plants with soapy water or pick the **pests** off by hand.

Birds nibble at young plants. But they also eat up **pests** like slugs and snails.

Ladybugs, frogs, and spiders are your friends. They feed on minibeast pests.

Caterpillar

Weeds are wild plants that can take over your garden.

They take the nutrients, water, and light that your plants need to grow.

Flowers such as daisies, buttercups, and dandelions are all **weeds**. But they do look pretty!

Dandelions

How can you stop slugs and snails that feed at night?

These minibeasts hate sharp things. So leave broken eggshells around your plants to stop them reaching the stems.

WHAT CAN I GROW?

Look out for ideas about healthy plants

Aunt Melissa looked sadly at her plant.

"What's the matter?" asked Chloe.

"Look at its leaves," said Aunt Melissa. "They're all yellow and droopy."

"Does it need more water?" asked Chloe.

Clara felt the soil. "Maybe it has too much water, or not enough light."

Chloe put the plant near the window. "The light will help it grow," she said.

24

"I think Aunt Melissa needs a plant that's easy to look after," said Clara.

"Perhaps you could help me," said Aunt Melissa. "Let's visit the botanical garden for some ideas."

"What's a botanical garden?" asked Chloe.
"It's where they grow all kinds of plants," said Clara.

An hour later, they arrived at the garden. Chloe and Clara spotted an enormous greenhouse. "A greenhouse helps you keep plants from hot countries," said Clara. "It keeps them warm."

They walked past a huge tree.
"Let's climb it!" said Clara.
"Look at its trunk!"
laughed Chloe.
"It's too tall!"

"Why don't you grow
a tree like this?" asked Clara.

"That tree is 200 years old,"
said Aunt Melissa.
"I'm not sure I want to wait that long!"

Next they looked at the flowers.
"Look at all those bright colors," said Chloe.

"The colors attract bees and butterflies," said Clara. "They carry pollen from one plant to another and help them grow new seeds."

"You could grow sunflowers," said Chloe.

"Look at their long stems!"

"I do love sunflowers," said Aunt Melissa. "But they are a bit tall. Let's keep looking."

Inside the first greenhouse was a little waterfall and a pond. "Why don't you grow water lilies," said Chloe. "You don't need to water them!"

"But I don't have a pond!" said Aunt Melissa.

The next greenhouse had a sign saying, "Rainforest Habitat."

"It's hot in here," said Chloe. "It's steamy too," said Clara.

"Lots of plants live together in a rainforest," said Aunt Melissa.

"A rainforest has all the hot sun and water they need."

"Wow! What are those?" asked Chloe.

"Look at the fruit. They must be banana plants," said Clara.

"Their huge leaves catch lots of light from the sun and use it to make food."

"They're a bit big to grow in my house," said Aunt Melissa.

"Can we get something to eat?" asked Chloe. "All these bananas are making me hungry."

On the way to the restaurant, Chloe spotted some very strange looking plants.

"Their leaves look like a big mouth," said Clara.

"They are a sort of mouth," said Aunt Melissa. "That's a Venus flytrap. It catches flies and takes the nutrients from their body."

"Yuck. I don't feel hungry anymore," said Chloe.

29

The last greenhouse was hot and dry. In the middle was a big cactus.

Chloe felt its prickly spines. "Ouch. They're sharp," she said.

"Does a cactus need much water?" asked Clara. "No," said Aunt Melissa.

"That's it!" said Chloe. "You should grow a cactus. "What a good idea," said Aunt Melissa. "A cactus sounds like an easy plant to look after!"

WRITE YOUR OWN STORY about plants. Or take a look at the plants in your house or school. See if you can list their different parts. Don't forget that fruit and vegetables come from plants too!

	Carrot	Cactus	Daffodil	Tomato plant	Oak tree
Stem	Short	Prickly	Long	Long/Thin	Trunk
Leaves	Bushy	Prickly	Long/Thin	✓	✓
Roots	Orange	Long	✓	✓	v. big!
Flowers	✘	Purple	Yellow	Yellow	✓
Fruit/Nut	✘	Pink	✘	Red	Acorn

QUIZ

Look at this plant.

What tells you it is not **healthy?**

What could you do to help it?

Answer on page 8

How would you measure
a growing plant?

Answer on page 13

What happens if you do not
water a plant? Why is too
much **water** bad for plants?

Answers on page 14

What are these plant parts called?

Answers on page 9, 11, 13, 26

INDEX